Knots & Splices

Steve Judkins and Tim Davison

fernhurst
B O O K S

D0242780

Copyright © Fernhurst Books 1998.

First published 1998 by Fernhurst Books, Duke's Path, High Street, Arundel,
West Sussex, BN18 9AJ, UK. Tel: 01903 882277 Fax: 01903 882715.

Write, phone or fax the publisher for a free, full-colour brochure.

Printed in China

British Library Cataloguing in Publication Data:
A catalogue record for this book is available from the British Library.

ISBN 1 898660 47 6

Cover design by Creative Byte.

Design & DTP by Creative Byte, Bournemouth.

The authors would like to thank Ken Yalden, Charlie Smith and Tim Field
of the International Guild of Knot Tyers for their kind assistance.

Contents

Welcome to
Knots and Splices

This little book begins with the ten knots everyone should know (pages 8 to 27). It then gives a further selection of useful knots. Finally, we show some splicing (joining ropes) and whipping (stopping the end unwinding).

Terms

Bend A bend joins two ropes.

Hitch A hitch is used to attach a rope to something else, eg a post.

Splice A splice is used to make an eye or a join without tying a knot. It works on friction. It doesn't weaken the rope as much as a knot.

Whipping A thin line used to stop a rope's end unlaying (unwinding).

Loop A complete turn, with a cross-over.

Bight An incomplete loop.

Stopper knot A knot which stops a rope being pulled through an eye.

Swedish fid A grooved spike for splicing rope.

Coil   To twist a rope into a series of loops.

Thimble A metal fitting put into an eye (to reduce wear).

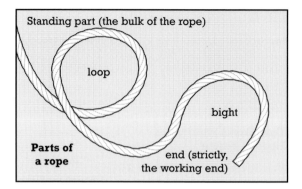

Standing part (the bulk of the rope)

loop

bight

Parts of a rope

end (strictly, the working end)

Knot basics

A half hitch is the start of many knots. So is a round turn.

Security

Length of tail Always work the knot tight, leaving a good tail.

Strength A knot reduces the strength of a rope. (Some knots may almost halve the strength).

Undoing a knot

Some knots can be capsized – eg a reef knot. Hold the standing part and pull back the nearest end. You can then slide the knot off the rope.

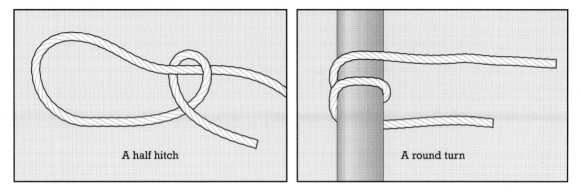

A half hitch

A round turn

ROPES
Ropes can be made from a range of materials. The table on page 6 lists some of these, and the ropes' properties.

Once the fibres have been chosen, they can be put together in a number of ways to make a rope. The most common ropes are *3-strand laid, 8-strand braid* and *core-plus-cover.*

Pre-stretched rope
The rope is stretched in the factory.
When you use it later, it won't stretch so much.

Wear
Wear causes broken fibres, or can even melt the fibres together. The trick is to lead ropes properly so they don't go round sharp corners. Be careful with core-plus-cover ropes: the strength is in the core, but it's hidden by the cover.

Sunlight
The ultra violet in sunlight is bad for ropes.

Measuring ropes
The thickness of a rope is given as the diameter in millimetres. (Ropes used to be measured around the circumference, in inches.)

Choosing a rope

1. First decide on the strength you need.
2. Then decide how much stretch you need.
3. Do you want the rope to float or sink?
4. Do you need a soft rope (for easy handling?)

What ropes are made from		
Type of fibre	**Name**	**What's the rope like?**
Synthetic	Nylon	Smooth. Stretchy. Very strong.
	Polyester & Terylene	Smooth. Stretches a little. Very strong. Common. Heavy.
	Polypropylene	Can be smooth or hairy. Floats. Cheap.
	Polyethylene Plastic	Floats. Weaker than Polypropylene. Cheap.
Exotics	Spectra Vectran	All the exotics are stronger than steel rope, size for size. All are expensive. All have very little stretch.
	Aramid	Aramid is not very good at bending and weakens when knotted. Doesn't wear well.
Natural	Manilla & Sisal	Cheap. Weaker than man-made fibre. Rots.

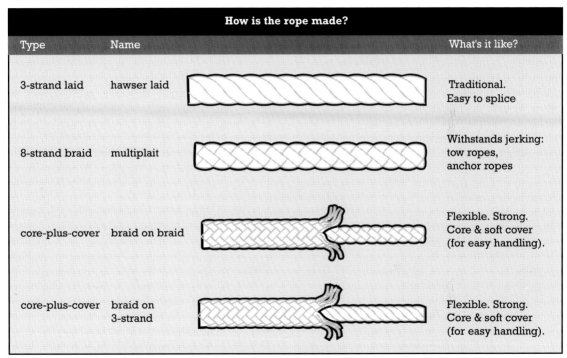

How is the rope made?			
Type	Name		What's it like?
3-strand laid	hawser laid		Traditional. Easy to splice
8-strand braid	multiplait		Withstands jerking: tow ropes, anchor ropes
core-plus-cover	braid on braid		Flexible. Strong. Core & soft cover (for easy handling).
core-plus-cover	braid on 3-strand		Flexible. Strong. Core & soft cover (for easy handling).

There are many alternative ways of tying the knots in this book. And most of the knots have alternative names! As you become more proficient, you will find your own preferred methods and names.

Round turn & two half hitches

Use: Attaching a rope to a ring or post.

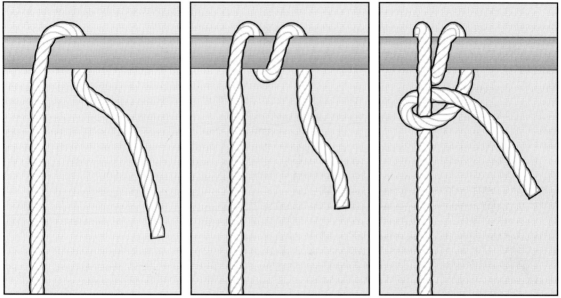

1. Pass the end round the object.

2. Take another complete turn.

3. Take the end over the standing part, around it and back through to form a half hitch.

4. Repeat, to form a second half hitch.

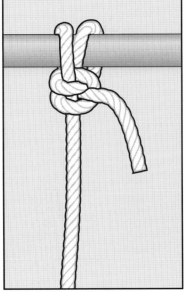

5. Pull tight.

 One of the most useful knots.

 Secure, if tied correctly and tightened up.

 Good for untying under pressure. Provided you keep tension on the end, the round turn will hold the loaded rope while you untie the half hitches.

Clove hitch

Use: Attaching a rope to a ring or post.

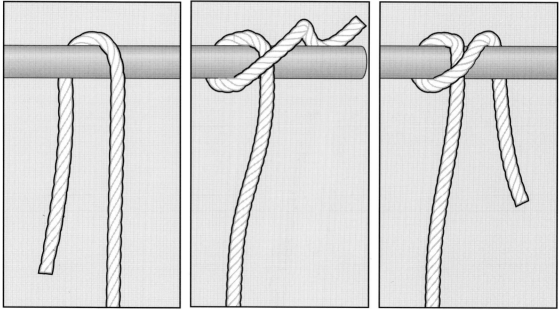

1. Pass the working end over the object...

2. ...and back over the standing part.

3. Pass the working end round the object.......

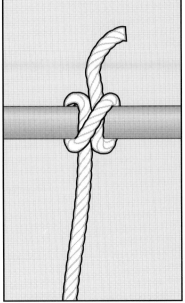

 Easy to undo.

 Must be an even pull,
on both ends.

 When the pull is from one
end only, the knot can slip
and work loose.

4. .....and back through the loop.

5. Pull tight.

Figure of eight

Use: As a stopper knot. Stops the end of a rope being pulled through a hole.

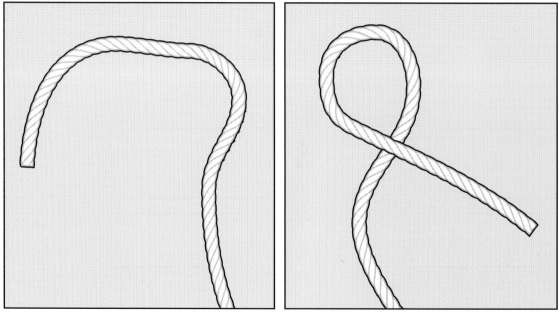

1. Make a bight.

2. Pass the end over the standing part to form a loop.

Easy to undo.

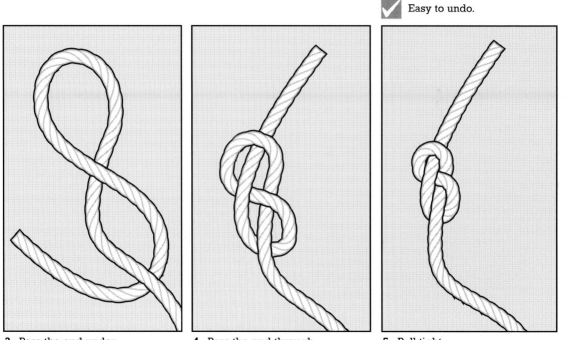

3. Pass the end under the standing part.

4. Pass the end through the top loop.

5. Pull tight.

Reef knot

Use: For tying the ends of a rope around an object, eg. a parcel, a bandage, the neck of a sack.

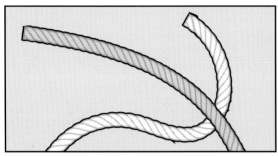

1. Keep working with the same end. Right over left.

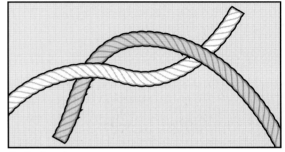

2. And under.

5. And under.

6. Pull tight and check.

Note: A bow is a reef knot, with steps 4,5 & 6 made from loops.

3. Carry on with the same end....

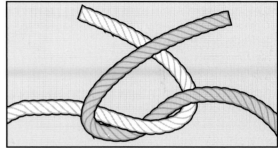

4. Left over right.

If one end snags, or only one end is pulled,
the knot can capsize and come undone.

Check you haven't tied a granny. This will slip.

Bowline

Use: Making a secure loop in a rope.

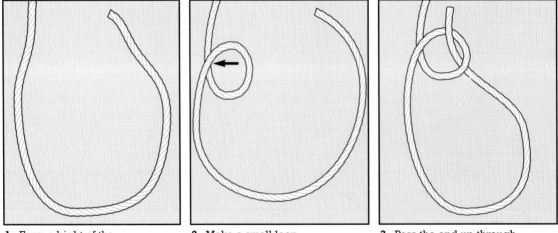

1. Form a bight of the required size.

2. Make a small loop.

 Check the loop is as shown.

3. Pass the end up through the small loop .....

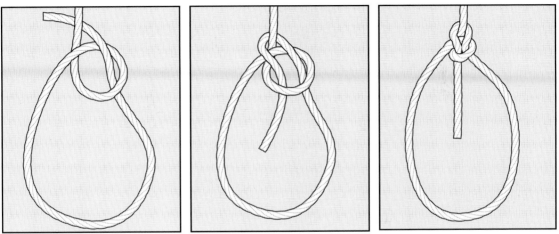

4. ...under the standing part.......

5. ....and down through the small loop.

6. Pull tight and check there is a long tail.

 You need a long tail.

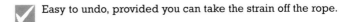 Easy to undo, provided you can take the strain off the rope.

Bowline on a bight
Use: A chair or a harness.

A secure knot. Can still be tied if there is no free end.
The working bight is the mid-part of the rope.

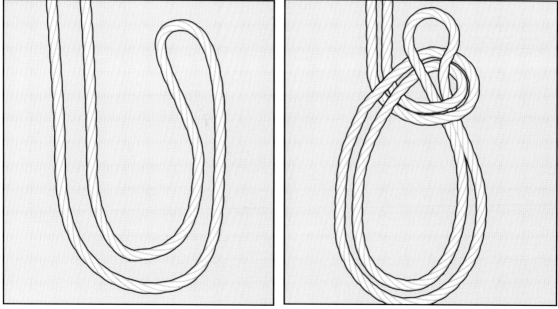

1. Form a bight.

2. Make a small loop and push the (doubled) end through.

Running bowline

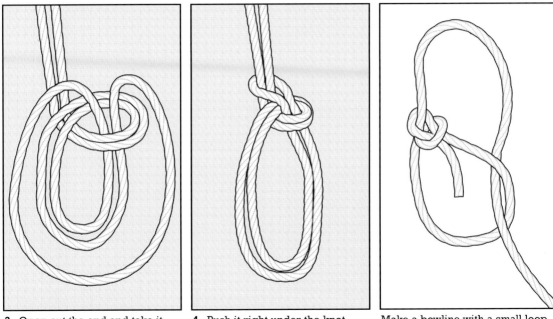

3. Open out the end and take it over the bottom of the knot.

4. Push it right under the knot.
5. Pull tight.

Make a bowline with a small loop. This loop runs on the standing part.

Sheet bend

Use: Joining two ropes of similar thickness.

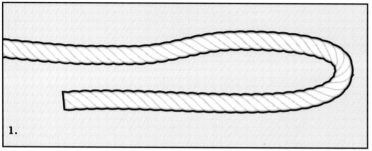

☠ Where the ropes are very different in thickness, use a double sheet bend....... see pages 22-23.

1. Make a bight in the thicker rope.

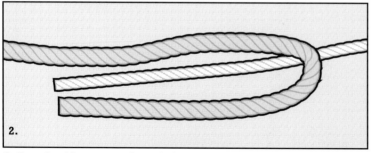

2. Pass the thinner rope through the bight .....

3. ....around and under, in the direction that will eventually leave both ends on the same side.

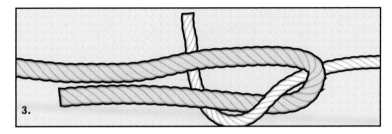

4. Pass the end of the thinner rope under its own standing part.

5. Pull tight. Double check that the loose ends are on the same side.

Double sheet bend

Use: A more secure version of the sheet bend.

 Check: Both ends must be on the same side

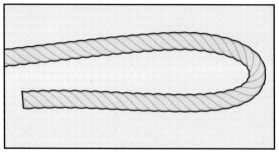

1. Make a bight in the thicker rope.

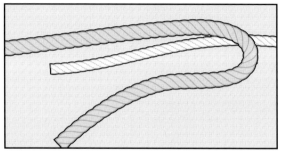

2. Pass the thinner rope through the bight.

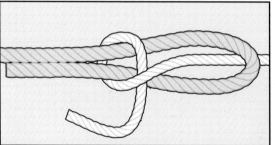

4. Complete a single sheet bend.

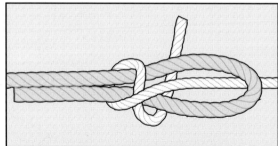

5. Pass the end under the thick rope again.

More secure than a single sheet bend.

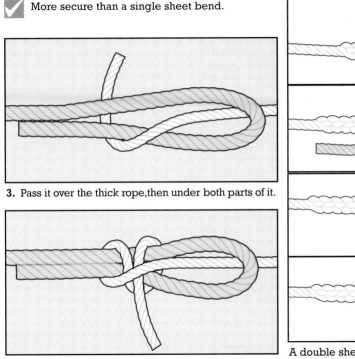

3. Pass it over the thick rope, then under both parts of it.

6. And under its own standing part.

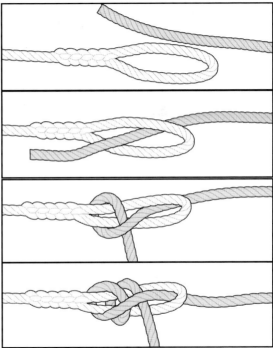

A double sheet bend can be used to join a rope (of any thickness) to a rope loop (becket).

Fisherman's bend/Anchor hitch

Use: Attaching a rope to a ring (eg on an anchor).

This knot is related to the round turn & two half hitches, but is more secure.

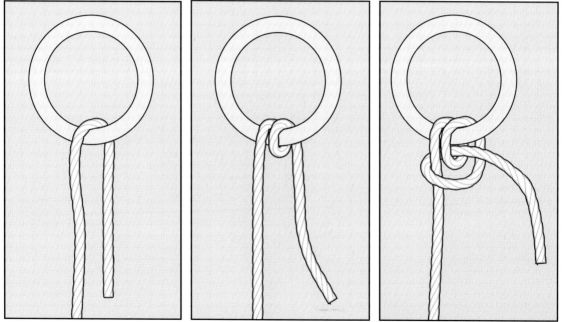

1. Pass the end through the ring.   **2.** Make another turn.   **3.** Pass the end through the turns.

Very secure.

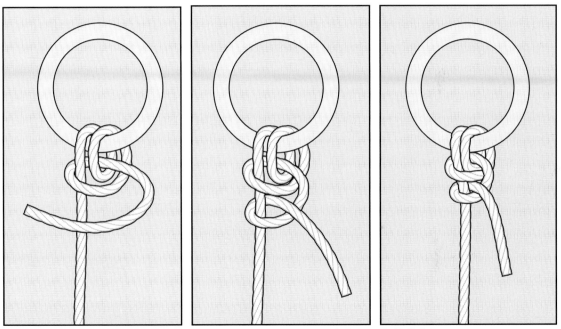

4. Then over the standing part.....

5. ...and under to make a half hitch.

6. Pull tight.

Rolling hitch

Use: To attach a line to a rod or
another rope so it grips it.
To pull a log.
To take the strain off a fouled rope.

1. Pass the end over
   the object.

2. Take it around the object
   and over itself.

3. Take it around the object and
   over itself again.

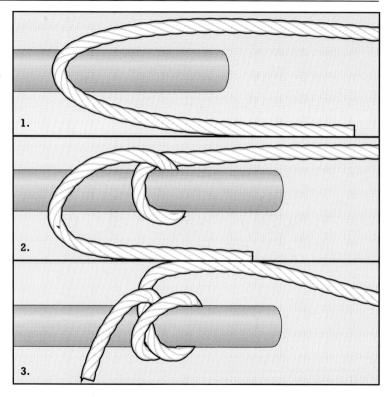

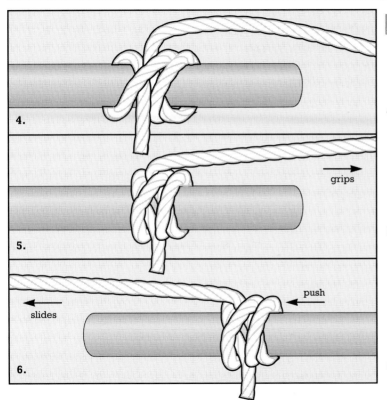

The knot only grips in one direction. Plan ahead, so it will grip when you pull.

4. Take the end around the object again and back under itself.

grips

5. The knot grips when pulled like this.

push

slides

6. The knot slides when pushed the other way.

Carrick bend

Use: For joining large ropes as well as small ones.

1. Make a loop.

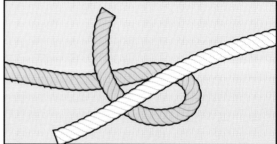

2. Pass the second rope over the loop.

5. Under.

6. Over.

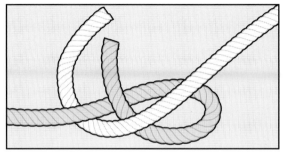

3. Under.

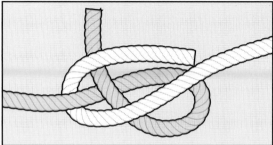

4. Over.

7. Under. For large ropes, complete by lashing the ends to the standing parts.

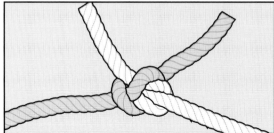

8. For small ropes, don't fix the ends. Instead pull until the knot flips, like this.

Sheepshank

Use: To shorten a rope temporarily. To protect a piece of chafed rope (chafed bit must be the centre of the 'Z').

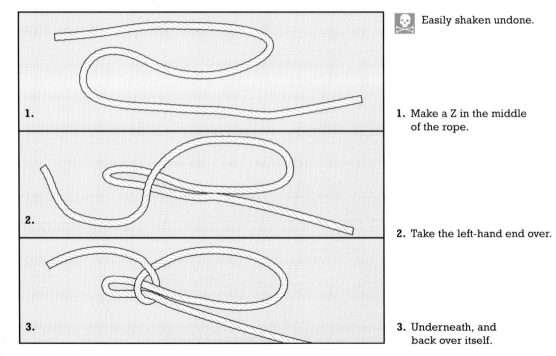

☠ Easily shaken undone.

1. Make a Z in the middle of the rope.

2. Take the left-hand end over.

3. Underneath, and back over itself.

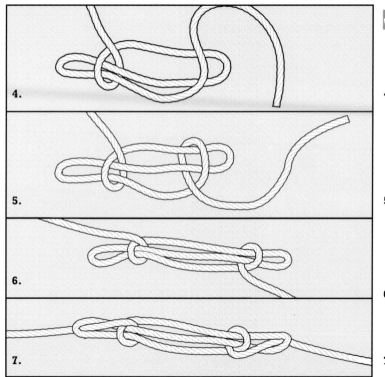

Step 7 shows how to make the knot secure, provided the ends are free to go through the loops.

4. Take the right-hand end over.

5. Underneath, and back over itself.

6. Pull tight.

7. For security, put each working end through its loop.

Constrictor knot

Use: To make a temporary whipping on a frayed rope. A binding e.g. to tie up the top of a sack.

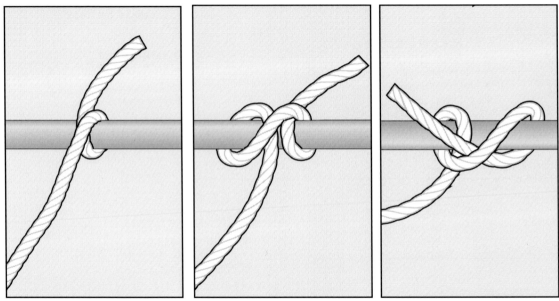

1. Take the end around the object and over itself.

2. Then around again and back under itself. You have tied a clove hitch.

3. Now take the end sideways, across the standing part.

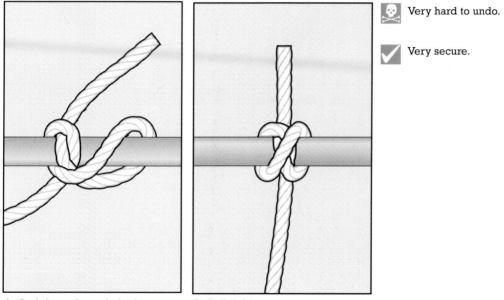

Very hard to undo.

Very secure.

4. And down through the loop. **5.** Pull tight.

Buntline hitch

Use: A safe knot for securing a rope to a ring or post.

 Very secure.   Not easy to undo

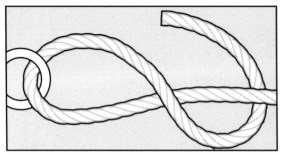

1. Pass the end through the ring and over then around the standing part.

2. Back over and under the standing part.

3. Complete a clove hitch.

4. Pull tight.

Surgeon's knot

Use: For tying the ends of a rope around an object, e.g. a parcel or a bandage.

Like a reef knot with an extra twist.
The extra twist helps hold the knot while tying the second part.

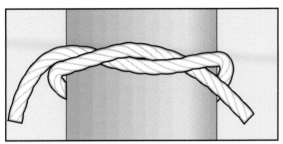

1. Right over left.

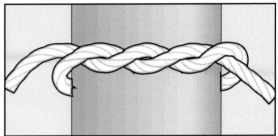

2. And again.

3. Left over right.

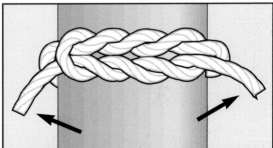

4. And again. Pull tight.

Alpine butterfly bend

Use: Joining two ropes securely.

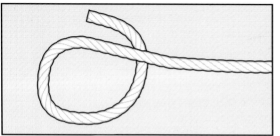

1. Make a loop with the end under the standing part.

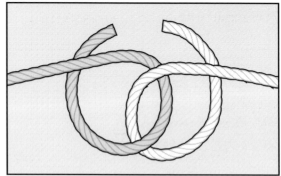

2. Take the second rope through the loop, round, and under its standing part.

3. Take both working ends down through the centre of the knot.

4. Pull tight.

Fisherman's knot/Englishman's knot
Use: Joining two ropes securely.

 For thin line.

 Difficult to undo.

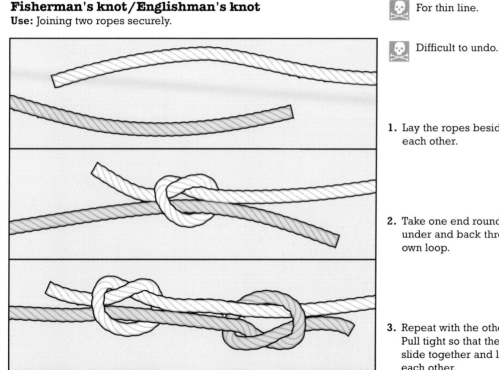

1. Lay the ropes beside each other.

2. Take one end round the other, under and back through it's own loop.

3. Repeat with the other end. Pull tight so that the two knots slide together and lock against each other.

Cow hitch

Use: To attach a rope to a peg or rod.

☠ Insecure, unless the free end is locked as in figure 4.

4.

For security, pass the end through both turns (to form a pedigree cow hitch).

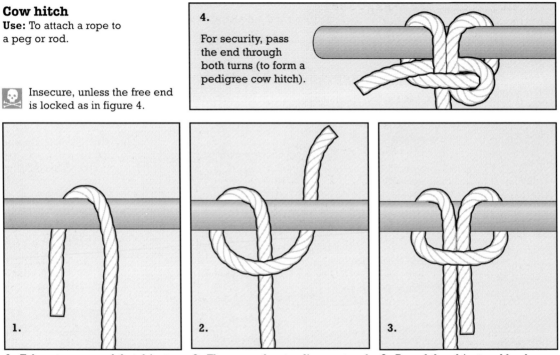

1. Take a turn around the object.

2. Then over the standing part and under the object.

3. Round the object and back through the loop.

Cow hitch round turn/Prusik knot

Use: To attach a rope to a pole. To help a climber climb up his safety rope. In this case he would use a small loop of rope, with a prusik knot tied in it around the safety rope. It slides up OK, but locks when he puts weight on it.

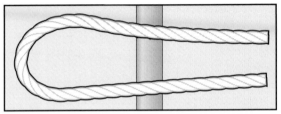

1. Make a bight in the middle of the rope.

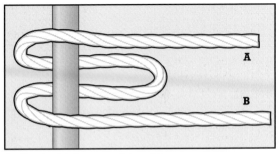

2. Put the bight around the object.

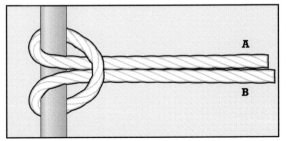

3. Put A and B through the bight.

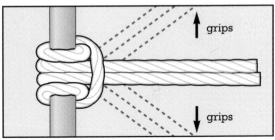

4. Take the bight around the object again and put A and B throught the bight again.

Timber hitch

Use: To lift or drag a long, round object.

 Easy to undo.

1. Put the end around the post and around the standing part.

2. Now make several twists with the lay of the rope.

3. Draw the hitch up tight.

4. For added security, go around the object again.

Marlinespike hitch

Use: Attaching a rod to a rope, mid-line, to use as a purchase.

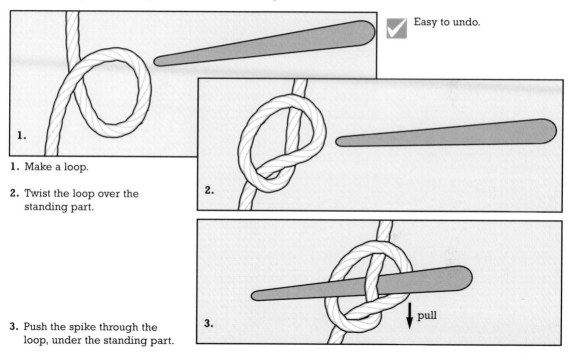

Easy to undo.

1. Make a loop.

2. Twist the loop over the standing part.

3. Push the spike through the loop, under the standing part.

pull

Manharness knot/ Artillery loop

Use: To make a handle in a rope (eg for pulling).

1. Make a loop in the middle of the line.

2. Slide the loop behind the standing part.

3. Take the top of the loop over the standing part and under the bottom of the loop.

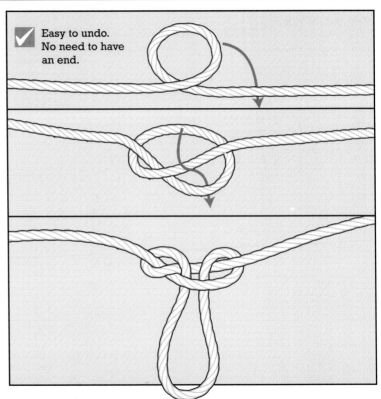

Easy to undo. No need to have an end.

Trucker's hitch /
Dolly knot
Use: Tying down.

✓ Gives a purchase.
Can be repeated along
the length of an object.

✓ Pulling the working end
undoes the series of knots.

☠ First loop can topple. Prevent
this by using two turns.

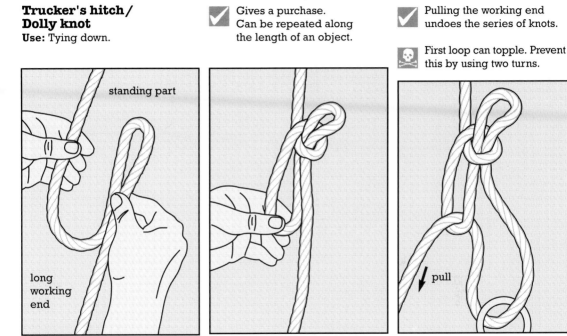

1. To tie down an object to a ring.
Make a bight.

2. Put the bight over the standing
part and roll. (You can go
round twice for safety).

3. Take the working end through
the ring and through the loop.
Pull to tension the standing part

Marling hitches
Use: Lashing a long bundle.

 Must go **over** in step 3, or the lashing will loosen.

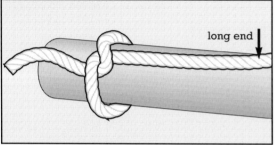

long end

1. The first hitch in place.

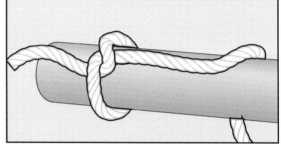

2. Take the working end around the object.

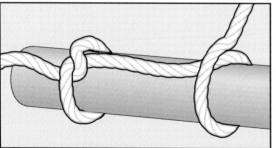

3. Over the standing part.

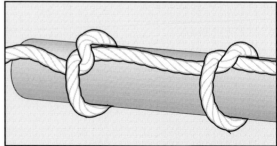

4. Then under. Repeat.

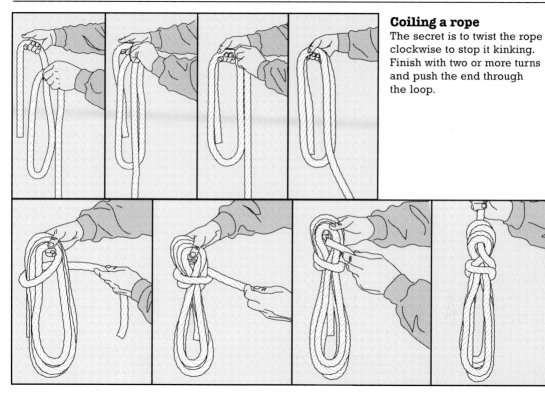

Coiling a rope

The secret is to twist the rope clockwise to stop it kinking. Finish with two or more turns and push the end through the loop.

Turk's head

Use: Along a tiller (to stop your hand slipping). For decoration. You can also make it flat for a mat.

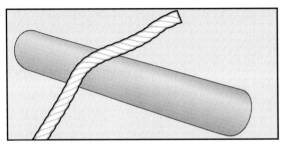

1. Take an end over the object.

2. Pass it around and over itself.

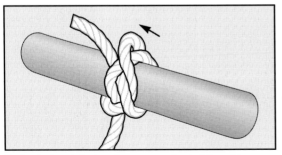

5. Push the right-hand turn over the left-hand turn.

6. Take the end over and under from left to right.

3. Around the object again.

4. Pass the working end over and back under the first turn.

7. Rotate the knot. Pass the end through the first loop, next to the standing part.

You can double or triple the knot by passing the end alongside all the original turns. Here it is doubled.

Eye splice

Use: For making a permanent eye in 3-strand rope.

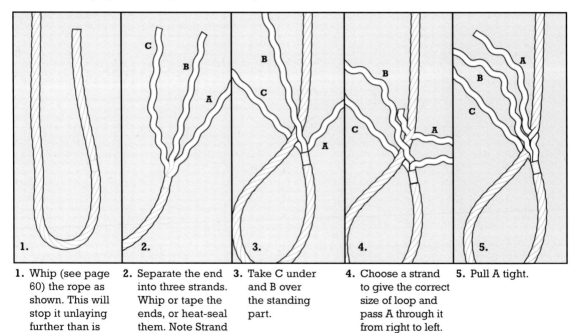

1. Whip (see page 60) the rope as shown. This will stop it unlaying further than is needed.

2. Separate the end into three strands. Whip or tape the ends, or heat-seal them. Note Strand B is on the top.

3. Take C under and B over the standing part.

4. Choose a strand to give the correct size of loop and pass A through it from right to left.

5. Pull A tight.

Reduces strength by 30%.

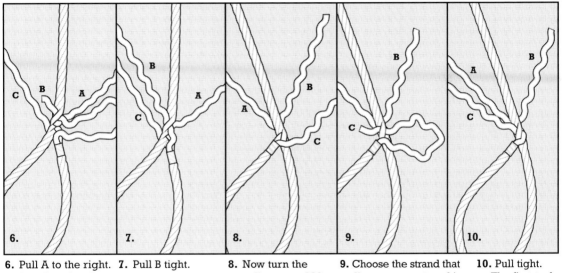

6. Pull A to the right. Pass B under the next strand up.

7. Pull B tight.

8. Now turn the splice over, 180 degrees.

9. Choose the strand that lies uppermost, and is below the two that have been tucked. Pass C under the strand, from right to left.

10. Pull tight. The first tuck is now complete.

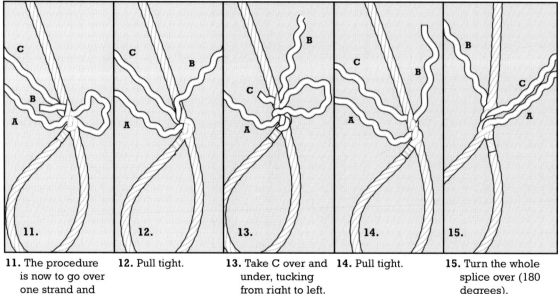

11. The procedure is now to go over one strand and under the next. Start with B and tuck from right to left.

12. Pull tight.

13. Take C over and under, tucking from right to left.

14. Pull tight.

15. Turn the whole splice over (180 degrees).

Reduces the strength by 30%.

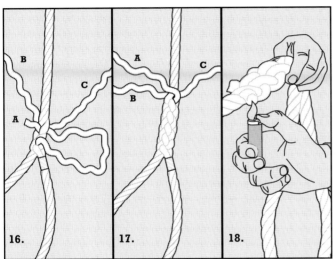

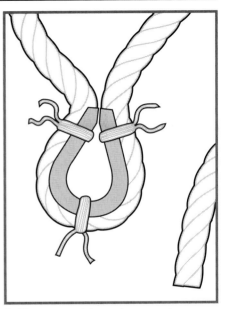

16. Take A over and under, tucking from right to left

17. Pull tight. Repeat B, C, A, to give five tucks. (For natural fibre only 3 tucks are needed.)

18. Synthetic rope: cut the ends quite close and heat-seal. Natural fibres: cut the ends quite long.

1. For wear resistance incorporate a thimble.
2. Choose one so the rope fits into it snugly.
3. Whip the rope tightly onto the thimble before you begin.

Short splice

Use: To join two pieces of identical 3-strand rope.

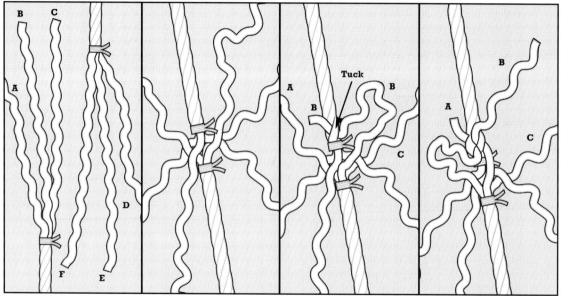

1. Prepare the ends by whipping and unlaying.

2. Interlock the ropes so the strands run alternatively.

3. Choose any strand, eg B. Make a tuck, from right to left.

4. Now pass A under the next strand, tucking from right to left.

The idea is to interlock the ropes, then splice them in a similar
way to the eye splice, with three tucks each side of the join.

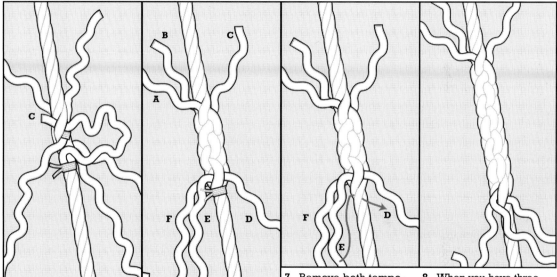

5. Turn the whole splice
upside down (180
degrees) and make a
tuck with C.

6. Continue tucking (over,
under) and rotating
until there are three
tucks with A, B & C.

7. Remove both tempo-
rary whippings. Splice
the other side, starting
with either D, E or F.
(Here it's E.)

8. When you have three
tucks on this side too,
cut the ends and heat-
seal them (synthetic
rope). For natural fibres
cut the ends quite long.

Eye in braid-on-braid rope

This is similar to the eye on pages 58-59. But the core is braided, not 3-strand. So the cover is pulled down the centre of the core.

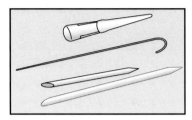

You will need a splicing kit:
a fid, a pusher/needle and two hollow needles.

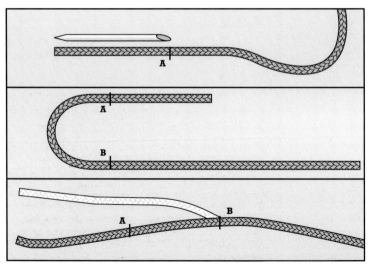

1. Tie a knot two metres from the end to stop the cover slipping. Cut off the heat-sealed end. Make a mark one needle-length from the end – mark A.

2. Make a bight the size of the eye required, and make mark B opposite A.

3. Pull out the core from B.

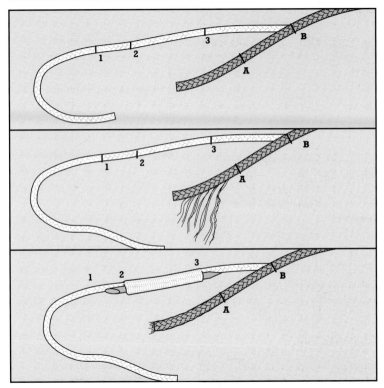

4. Mark the core where it comes out of the cover: mark 1. Pull out more core. One short needle-length from 1, make mark 2. One long needle-length, make mark 3.

5. Reduce the thickness of the cover by pulling out threads and cutting off.

6. Push the needle up the core from mark 2 to mark 3.

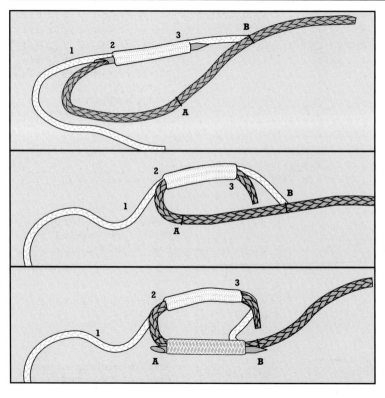

7. Put the (thinned) cover end into the needle.

8. Use a pusher to push the cover through.

9. Push the needle through from mark A to mark B.

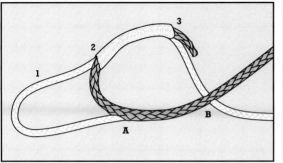

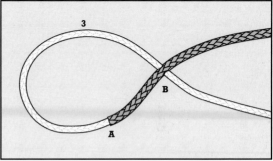

10. Push the core through using a pusher.

11. Pull both ends until you've smoothed the crossover point.

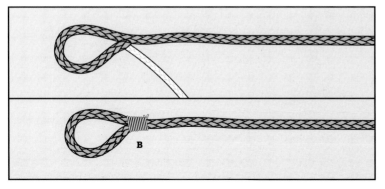

12. 'Milk' the cover back from the knot to the splice. The core will disappear into it.

13. Cut off the loose core at an angle and 'milk' it back in.

14. Put a whipping round point B.

Eye in braid-on-3-strand rope

You are going to make an eye by passing the core, and then the cover, up inside the rope's cover.
You will need your splicing kit (see page 54).

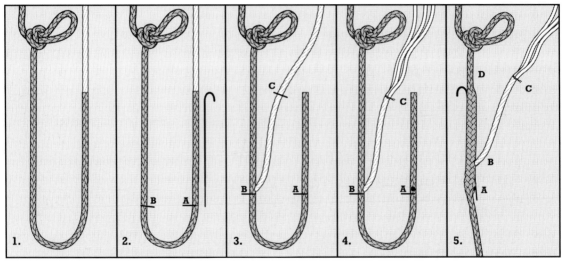

1. Tie a stopper knot 2 metres (6ft) from the end. Pull back the cover to expose 20cm (8in) of core. Milk the slack in the cover down to the stopper knot.
2. Measure one needle-length and mark the cover at A. Form the eye and make a mark B.

3. Make a hole at B and pull out the core. Whip the core at C so that C B = A B.
4. Unravel the core to the whipping and cut off 50% of each strand. Make a hole at A.
5. Milk the cover .... Turn the rope over. Go back

nearly a needle's-length from B and push a fid into the cover at D. Use it to push the needle through the cover from D, to come out at A.

8. Insert the needle 3 inches below D and out at B (making sure the needle is on the opposite side to the core tail).

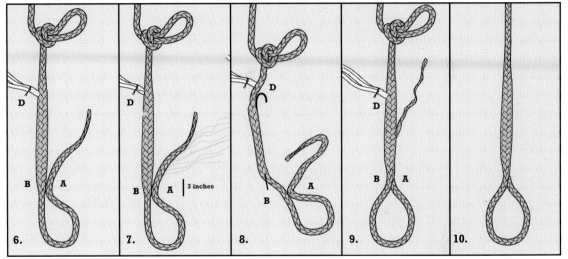

6. Thread the reduced ends of the core through the needle. Withdraw the needle so the core is pulled through the cover and out at D. This forms the eye.

7. Take 7 yarns out of the tail of the cover 3 inches from A and cut them off to make the tail thinner.

9. Pull the thinned cover through the thick cover until the tail comes out. Pull tight.

10. Cut off both tails (core and sheath) and milk until both ends are lost in the cover.

Common whipping

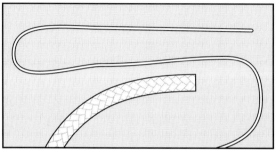

1. Make a bight in the whipping twine.

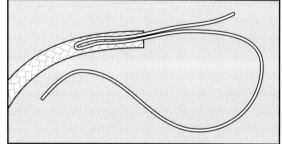

2. Lay the bight along the end of the rope.

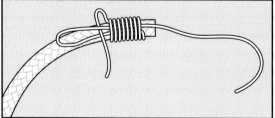

5. Push the end of the whipping twine through the loop.

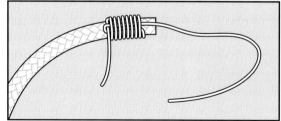

6. Pull the end of the whipping twine until tight.

This is a quick way of whipping. Make it neat and tight or it will not be secure.

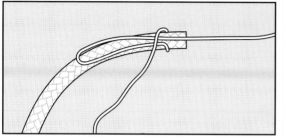

3. Begin to wrap the long end of the whipping twine around the rope and loop, working away from the rope's end. Keep the twine neat and tight.

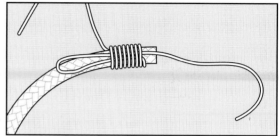

4. Keep winding until the whipping is 2.5 cm (1 inch) long.

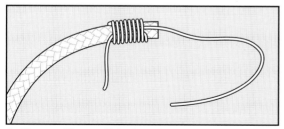

7. Keep pulling until the loop has been pulled halfway under the whipping.

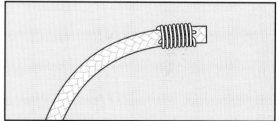

8. Pull very tight. Cut off both loose ends.

Sailmaker's whipping

Use: For three-strand rope.

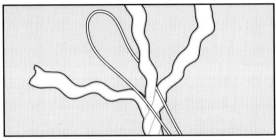

1. Unlay part of the rope. Make a bight in the whipping twine. Put it over the centre strand.

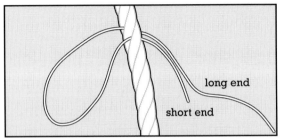

long end

short end

2. Re-lay the rope carefully, to grip the bight.

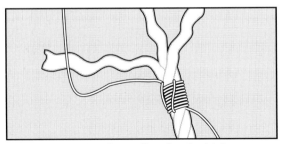

5. Pull tight on the short tail so that the bight clamps tight over the turns of the whipping.

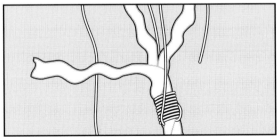

6. Turn the rope over, 180 degrees. Take the short end and with it follow the strand it is beside. Pass the end through the splayed rope.

Use: To make a sailmaker's whipping on braided ropes use a needle to thread the twine through the rope.

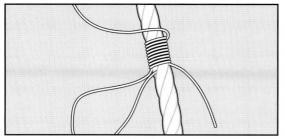

3. Wind the long end of the whipping twine around the rope, against the lay, for 2.5 cm (1 inch).

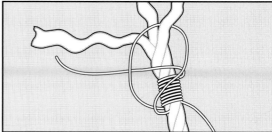

4. Follow the strand the bight is around, through the whipping. Put the loop over the end of the strand.

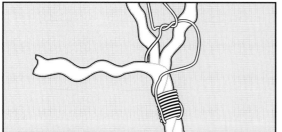

7. Tie a very tight reef knot in the ends of the whipping twine. Check the whipping is symmetrical.

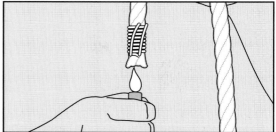

8. Cut off all the loose ends and heat-seal (see p. 64). For natural fibres leave longer ends.

Heat-sealing the end of a synthetic rope

Sometimes called the Butane Backsplice! **Use:** Heat-sealing can be used as a temporary whipping. But after a while the melted rope cracks. **Objective:** To melt the rope, not burn it!

 Don't touch the melted rope. Don't let melted rope drip on you.

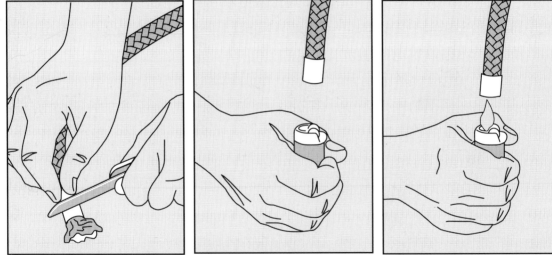

1. Tape the end. Then cut off the end, through the tape.

2. You are going to use a naked flame. Hold the lighter vertical. Light the flame with the rope well clear.

3. Rotate the rope as you lower it towards the flame, so the whole end is warmed. Don't lower too far, or the rope will burn.